Teacher's Resource Blackline Masters

CONTENTS

Dear Family,

Welcome to Kindergarten.

This is an especially exciting time for your child, and I'd like you to join me in making this a year of learning and fun. One of the things I'll be asking you to do is share information that will help me get to know your child better.

Throughout the year, I'll be sending home ideas for activities that you can do with your child to reinforce what we're learning in school. Please become involved as much as you can. Studies have shown that children who get support at home in reading and learning do better in school.

Here are two suggestions for things to do at home:

- **Read and discuss books with your child.** Even after children have learned to read on their own, there are many benefits to reading aloud to your child—and to letting your child read to you. Visit the library together so you can choose books that both of you will enjoy.

- **Let your child see you reading.** It's important to show your child that you think reading is valuable and enjoyable.

One other thing: I always appreciate having adult volunteers assist with classroom activities. If you can give some time in the classroom or at home with preparation, please let me know.

Thanks for working with me as a partner in your child's education. Together, we can help your child have a successful year!

Sincerely,

_____

Estimada familia:

¡Bienvenidos a kindergarten!

Esta es una ocasión muy especial para todos. Mi deseo es que juntos podamos hacer de éste un año productivo y divertido. Una de las cosas que les voy a pedir es que compartan conmigo información acerca de su niño o niña. Esa información me ayudará a conocer mejor a los niños.

Durante el año escolar, les enviaré cartas con ideas de actividades que pueden hacer juntos en casa. Esas actividades ayudarán a complementar lo que aprendemos en clase. Por favor, colaboren tanto como puedan. Estudios han demostrado que los niños que reciben apoyo en sus casas siguen mejor en la escuela.

A continuación hay dos sugerencias importantes de actividades que pueden hacer en casa:

- **Lean libros juntos y hablen de lo que leen.** Aunque los niños ya sepan leer, es muy beneficioso que usted les lea libros en voz alta y también que ellos lean en voz alta para los demás. Vayan a la biblioteca y escojan libros que les gusten a ambos.

- **Asegúrense de que su niño o niña lo vea leer a usted.** Es importante que usted demuestre que la lectura es importante y divertida.

Otra cosa importante: Yo siempre aprecio la ayuda que puedan prestar voluntarios adultos con las actividades de la clase. Por favor, avísenme si me pueden ayudar en el salón de clases, o en su casa, con detalles relacionados a la preparación de actividades.

Les agradezco de antemano por participar en la educación de su niño o niña. Juntos podemos ayudarle a tener un año muy exitoso.

Atentamente,

_____

A B C D E F G

H I J K L M N

O P Q R S T U

V W X Y Z

a b c d e f g

h i j k l m n

o p q r s t u

v w x y z

I can write
my name.

Today is my
birthday.

I can count
to 20.

I learned
my ABC's.

I read a
new book.

Place a Blackline Master picture for a Center (p.8) here. Write the names of children assigned to the center on the list or have children sign in. Post the list near the Center. Keep the sheet for your records.

My Journal

Name

Newsletter

Dear Family,

Throughout the school year children will hear classic stories in two formats, Read Aloud stories and Big Books in our reading themes. For the next few weeks, our reading theme will be *Look at Us!*

Look at Us!

Theme-Related Activities to Do Together

Learning the Alphabet

Take turns saying letters of the alphabet with your child. Vary the activity by occasionally clapping once instead of saying the next letter, and let your child say it. Write letters on pieces of paper, and have your child select and name the letters.

Reading Your Child's First Name

Help your child recognize his or her first name printed with an initial capital letter followed by lowercase letters. Print the name once, making headline-size letters and naming the letters as you write. Then have your child name the letters with you.

Reading Your Child's Last Name

Follow a similar procedure for helping your child read his or her last name. Then ask your child to circle and name letters in his or her name found in large advertisements.

Theme-Related Books to Enjoy Together!

Shape Space *by Catheryn Falwell. Clarion 1992 (32p)* A young gymnast dances her way among rectangles, triangles, and squares.

What Do You Like? *by Michael Grejniec. North-South 1992 (32p) also paper* A boy and girl take turns telling about the things they like. Available in Spanish as *¿Qué te gusta?*

The Body Book *by Shelley Rotner and Stephen Calcagnino. Orchard 2000 (32p)* Photos and simple text show that different parts of the body help us smell flowers, taste pizza, listen to friends, and run and jump.

My Five Senses *by Aliki. Simon 1994 (32p)* An introduction to sound, taste, smell, sight, and touch, the senses that help us discover and understand the world. Available in Spanish as *Mis cinco sentidos.*

Career Day *by Anne Rockwell. Harper 2000 (32p)* On Career Day, Mrs. Madoff's class learns about the different work that people of all ages do.

Mr. Brown Can Moo. Can You? *by Dr. Seuss. Random 1970 (48p)* From a cow's *moo* to a clock's *tick tock*, Mr. Brown can imitate all kinds of sounds.

Boletín

¡Mira como somos!

Estimada familia:

Durante el año escolar los niños escucharán historias tradicionales en dos formatos, como lectura en voz alta (Read Aloud stories) y como libros grandes (Big Books) en los temas de lectura. Durante las próximas semanas, estudiaremos el tema ¡Mira como somos!

Actividades para hacer juntos

Para aprender el alfabeto

Tomen turnos para decir el alfabeto. Para variar la actividad, dé palmadas ocasionalmente en vez de decir la letra y permita que su niño o niña la diga. Escriba letras en pedacitos de papel y pida que escoja y nombre las letras.

La lectura del nombre

Ayude a su niño o niña a reconocer su propio nombre escrito con la letra inicial en mayúscula y el resto de las letras en minúscula. Escriba el nombre con letras grandes y pronuncie cada letra mientras la escribe. Luego lean las letras juntos.

La lectura del apellido

Para leer el apellido, siga los mismos pasos que siguieron para la actividad anterior. Luego pida a su niño o niña que haga círculos alrededor de las letras de su apellido cuando las vea en titulares del periódico o de revistas

Libros relacionados al tema que pueden leer juntos

Shape Space *por Catheryn Falwell. Clarion 1992 (32p)* Una joven gimnasta baila entre rectángulos, triángulos y cuadrados.

What Do You Like? *por Michael Grejniec. North-South 1992 (32p) disponible como libro de bolsillo* Un niño y una niña se turnan para decir lo que le gusta a cada uno. Disponible en español con el título *¿Qué te gusta?*

The Body Book *por Shelley Rotner and Stephen Calcagnino. Orchard 2000 (32p)* Fotos y texto sencillo demuestran que diferentes partes del cuerpo nos ayudan a oler flores, saborear pizza, escuchar a los demás y correr y saltar.

My Five Senses *por Aliki. Simon 1994 (32p)* Una introducción al sonido, el gusto, el olfato, la vista y el tacto, los cinco sentidos que nos ayudan a descubrir y entender el mundo. Disponible en español con el título *Mis cinco sentidos.*

Career Day *por Anne Rockwell. Harper 2000 (32p)* La clase de la Sra. Madoff aprende acerca de los distintos trabajos que hacen personas de todas las edades.

Mr. Brown Can Moo. Can You? *por Dr. Seuss. Random 1970 (48p)* El señor Brown puede imitar todo tipo de sonidos, del *mugir* de una vaca al *tic-tac* del reloj.

Theme 1

Name _____ Date _____

	Beginning	Developing	Proficient
Listening Comprehension • Participates in shared and choral reading			
• Listens to a story attentively			
Phonemic Awareness • Recognizes rhyming words			
• Recognizes syllables in spoken words			
Letter Recognition • Recognizes letters			
• Matches capital and lowercase letters			
Concepts of Print • Understands left to right			
• Understands top to bottom			
Reading • Tells a story from a wordless picture book			
Comprehension • Compares and contrasts story elements			
• Notes important details			
Writing and Language • Can form letters			
• Writes own name			
• Draws and labels images			

For each child, write check marks or notes in the appropriate columns.

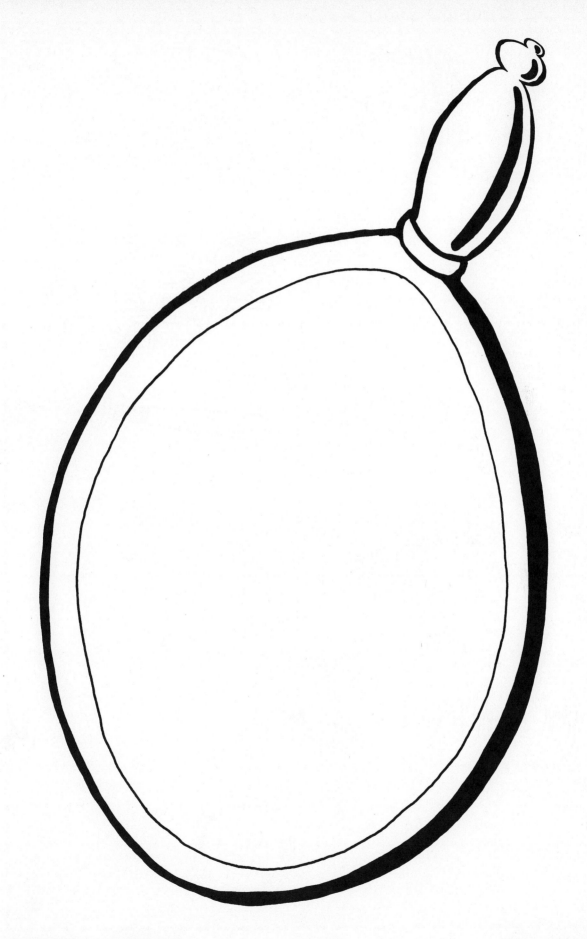

2

My Tiny Rhyme Book

1

3

4

6

5

7

8

My Journal

Name _____

Story retelling props for *The Gingerbread Man*

Story retelling props for *The Gingerbread Man*

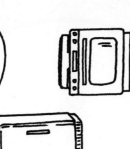

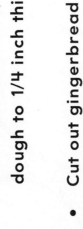
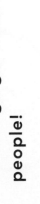

Directions:

- Cream shortening with sugar and molasses.

- Mix in rest of the ingredients.

- Put in refrigerator for 2 hours.

- Heat oven to 350°.

- On a floured board, roll dough to 1/4 inch thick.

- Cut out gingerbread people!

- Bake 10 to 12 minutes.

- Use raisins and frosting to make eyes, nose, a mouth!

- 1/3 cup shortening

- 1 1/2 cups molasses

- 1 cup brown sugar

- 2/3 cup water

- 7 cups flour

- 2 teaspoons baking powder

- 1 teaspoon salt

- 1/2 teaspoon allspice

- 1 1/2 teaspoons ginger

- 1 teaspoon cloves

- 2 teaspoons cinnamon

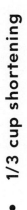
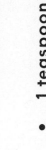

Story retelling props for The City Mouse and the Country Mouse

Story retelling props for *The City Mouse and the Country Mouse*

Story retelling props for *Mice Squeak, We Speak*

Story retelling props for *Mice Squeak, We Speak*

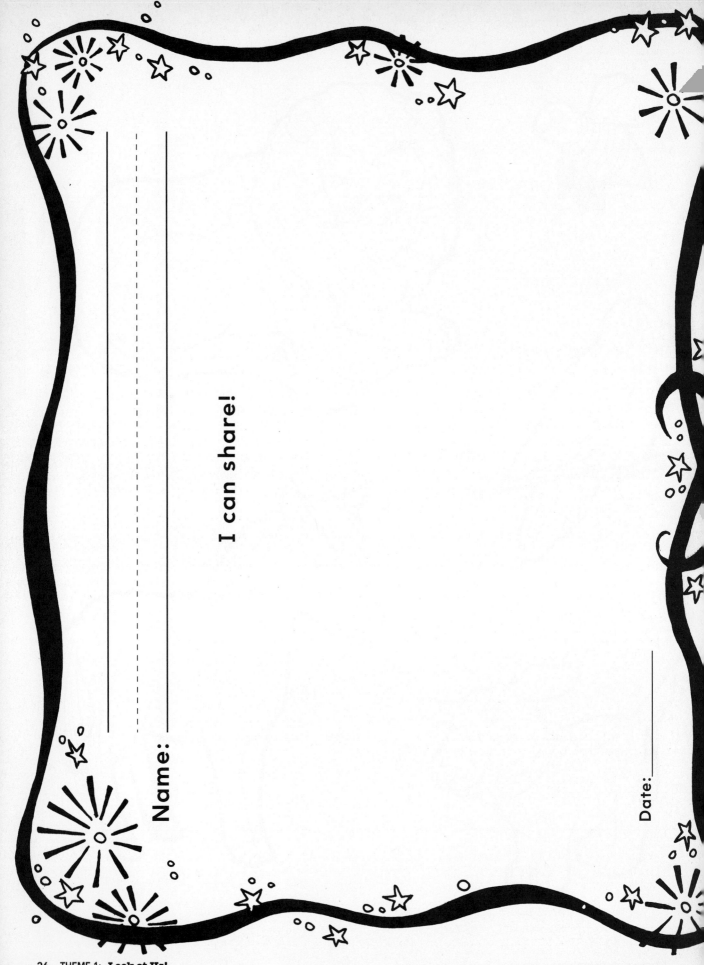

I can share!

Name: _____

Date: _____

Newsletter

Colors All Around

Dear Family,

For the next few weeks, our classroom reading theme will be *Colors All Around*. Children will listen to stories about colors. They will work on recognizing and writing the letters *s*, *m*, and *r* and identifying the sounds they represent.

Theme-Related Activities to Do Together

For the letters *Ss*

Shape the letter *s* with a piece of string and have your child identify it. Then print capital and lower case *s* and ask your child to identify them. Name a word that begins with *s*, and help your child name other words that begin with *s*.

For the letters *Mm*

Print a capital and lower case *m*. Have your child name the letters. Say, "Mary cooks meatballs. The words *Mary* and *meatballs* begin with the sound the letter *m* stands for." Help your child name other words that begin with *m*.

For the letters *Rr*

Print both capital and lower case *r* and ask your child to identify them. Say, "I'm going to say two words that begin with the sound the letter *r* stands for: *rabbit ran*." Help your child name other words that begin with *r*.

Theme-Related Books to Enjoy Together!

Mouse Paint *by Ellen Stoll Walsh. Harcourt 1989 (32p) also paper* Three white mice experiment mixing jars of red, yellow, and blue paint. Available in Spanish *as Pinta ratones.*

Who Said Red? *by Mary Serfozo. McElderry 1988 (32p) also paper* As his sister suggests colors he might like, a boy searches for his red kite in this rhyming story.

Mr. Rabbit and the Lovely Present *by Charlotte Zolotow. Harper 1962 (32p) also paper* A rabbit helps a girl create a colorful birthday gift for her mother. Available in Spanish as *El señor Conejo y el hermoso regalo.*

Kente Colors *by Debbi Chocolate. Walker 1996 (32p) also paper* A celebration of the colorful, traditional kente cloth made by the people of Ghana and Togo.

Harold and the Purple Crayon *by Robert Kraus. Harper 1955 (64p) also paper* A boy draws himself exciting adventures with a purple crayon. Available in Spanish as *Harold y el lápiz color morado.*

Planting a Rainbow *by Lois Ehlert. Harcourt 1988 (32p) also paper* Planting a garden of flowers, a child learns the colors of the rainbow.

Boletín

Rodeados de color

Estimada familia:

Durante las próximas semanas, trataremos el tema *Rodeados de color*. Los niños escucharán historias acerca de los colores. También aprenderán a reconocer y a escribir las letras *s*, *m* y *r*, y a identificar los sonidos que representan esas letras.

Actividades para hacer juntos

Para la letra *Ss*

Con un cordel, forme la letra *s* y pida a su niño o niña que la identifique. Luego escriba la *s* máyuscula y minúscula y pídale que las identifique. Diga una palabra con *s* inicial y ayude a su niño o niña a nombrar otras palabras que comiencen con la *s*.

Para la letra *Mm*

Escriba la *m* máyuscula y minúscula y pida a su niño o niña que las lea en voz alta. Diga: "María come maíz. Las palabras *María* y *maíz* comienzan con el sonido de la letra *m*". Ayude a su niño o niña a nombrar otras palabras que comienzan con la letra *m*.

Para la letra *Rr*

Escriba la letra *r* en máyuscula y en minúscula y pida a su niño o niña que las lea en voz alta. Diga: "Voy a decir dos palabras que comienzan con el sonido de la letra *r*: *río rocoso*". Ayude a su niño o niña a nombrar otras palabras que comiencen con la letra *r*.

Libros relacionados al tema que pueden leer juntos

Mouse Paint *por Ellen Stoll Walsh. Harcourt 1989 (32p) disponible como libro de bolsillo* Tres ratoncitos blancos mezclan envases de pintura roja, amarilla y azul. Disponible en español con el título *Pinta ratones*.

Who Said Red? *por Mary Serfozo. McElderry 1988 (32p) disponible como libro de bolsillo* En este cuento de rima, un niño busca su cometa roja mientras su hermana le sugiere distintos colores.

Mr. Rabbit and the Lovely Present *por Charlotte Zolotow. Harper 1962 (32p) disponible como libro de bolsillo* Un conejo ayuda a una niña a crear un colorido regalo para su mamá. Disponible en español con el título *El señor Conejo y el hermoso regalo*.

Kente Colors *por Debbi Chocolate. Walker 1996 (32p) disponible como libro de bolsillo* Este libro es una celebración de la tradicional y colorida tela "kente," hecha en Ghana y Togo.

Harold and the Purple Crayon *por Robert Kraus. Harper 1955 (64p) disponible como libro de bolsillo* Un niño dibuja grandes aventuras con un creyón morado. Disponible en español con el título *Harold y el lápiz color morado*.

Planting a Rainbow *por Lois Ehlert. Harcourt 1988 (32p) disponible como libro de bolsillo* Al sembrar un jardín de flores, un niño aprende los colores del arco iris.

Theme 2

Name _____   Date _____

	Beginning	Developing	Proficient
Listening Comprehension • Participates in shared and choral reading			
• Listens to a story attentively			
Phonemic Awareness • Can identify beginning sounds			
• Can identify syllables in spoken words			
Phonics • Can recognize initial sounds for *s, m, r*			
Concepts of Print • Recognizes use of capital at the beginning of a sentence			
• Can identify end punctuation			
Reading • Can read wordless stories			
• Can read the high-frequency words *I, see*			
Comprehension • Recognizes sequence of events			
• Can make inferences/ predictions			
Writing and Language • Can write simple words			
• Can participate in shared and interactive writing			

For each child, write check marks or notes in the appropriate columns.

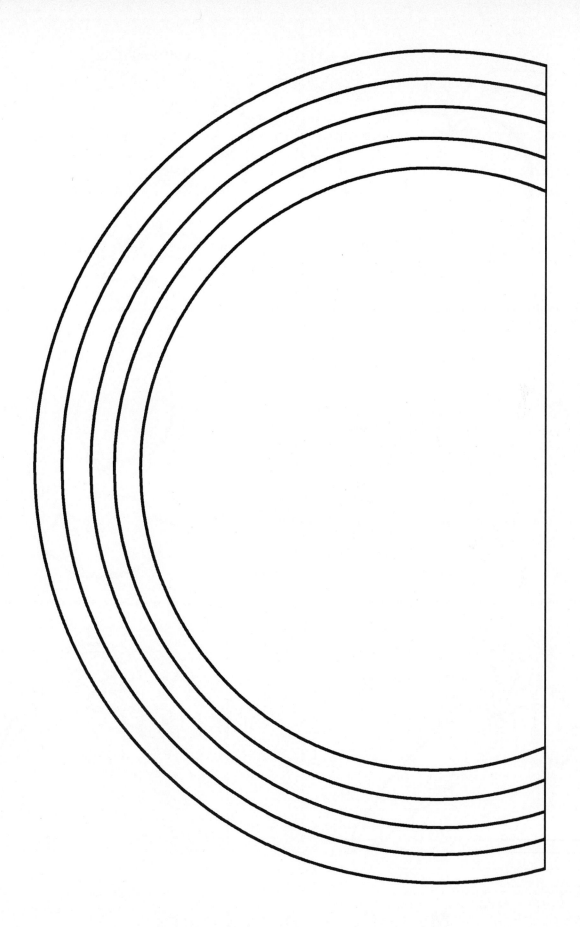

My Little Book of Colors

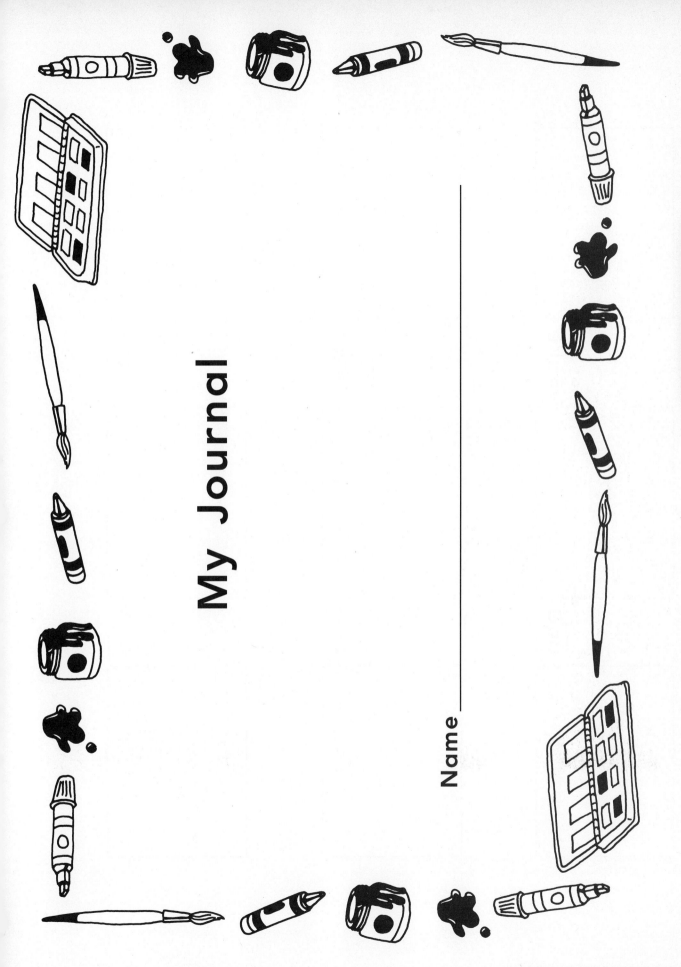

My Journal

Name

make

make

make

and

and

and

Name: _____

I went walking.

What did you see?

I saw a _____.

Name: _____

My Reading Log

I can read

My new words

_____   _____

- - - - - - - - - - - - - -   - - - - - - - - - - - - - -

_____   _____

Scales	Skin

Fur	Feathers

Name: _____

I love colors,
Yes I Do!

I can follow directions!

Name: _____

Date: _____

Newsletter

We're a Family

Dear Family,

Our next reading theme will be *We're a Family.* The Read Aloud and Big Book stories tell about families of animals and people. Children will focus on recognizing and writing the letters *t*, *b*, and *n* and learning the sound each letter represents.

Theme-related Activities to Do Together

For the letters *Tt*

Print capital *T* and lower case *t* and have your child identify the letters. Say, "*Tom* is a name that begins with the sound the letter *t* stands for." Help your child think of other names that begin with *t*.

For the letters *Bb*

Print both capital and lower case *b* for your child, and ask him or her to identify them. As you roll a ball to your child, say the name of a word that begins with the sound *b* stands for. Challenge your child to do likewise.

For the letters *Nn*

Print capital and lower case *n* and have your child identify the letters. Say, "I have nine noodles. *Nine* and *noodles* begin with the sound the letter *n* stands for." Collaborate with your child in naming words that begin with *n*.

Theme-related Books to Enjoy Together!

Katy No-Pocket *by Emmy Payne. Houghton 1944 (32p)* Pocketless Katy Kangaroo sets out to find something in which to carry her son Freddy. Available in Spanish as *Katy no tiene bolsa.*

Lots of Dads *by Shelley Rotner. Dial 1997 (32p)* Photos show all kinds of dads engaged in activities from work to play with their children.

Peter's Chair *by Ezra Jack Keats. Harper 1967 (32p) also paper* Peter learns to accept—and even to love—his new baby sister. Available in Spanish as *La silla de Pedro.*

Buzz *by Janet S. Wong. Harcourt 2000 (32p)* A busy morning for a boy and his parents begins with the alarm clock's buzz.

A Birthday Basket for Tia *by Pat Mora. Simon 1992 (32p) also paper* Cecilia prepares a special gift in honor of her great aunt's birthday. Available in Spanish as *Una canasta de cumpleaños para Tía.*

On Mother's Lap *by Ann Herbert Scott. Clarion 1992 (32p) also paper* An Inuit boy discovers there's room for himself and his baby sister on their mother's lap.

Boletín

Nuestra familia

Estimada familia:

Nuestro próximo tema será *Nuestra familia*. Las historias para leer en voz alta y las de los libros grandes son acerca de familias de animales y de personas. Los niños aprenderán a reconocer y escribir las letras *t*, *b* y *n*, y en identificar los sonidos que repesentan esas letras.

Actividades para hacer juntos

Para la letra *Tt*

Escriba la letra *T* mayúscula y minúscula, y pida a su niño o niña que identifique las letras. Diga: "*Tomás* es un nombre que comienza con el sonido de la letra *t*". Ayude a su niño o niña a pensar en otros nombres que comiencen con la *t*.

Para la letra *Bb*

Escriba la letra *b* en mayúscula y en minúscula, y pida a su niño o niña que las identifique. Mientras hace rodar una pelota hacia su niño o niña, diga una palabra que comience con el sonido de la letra *b*. Anime a su niño a hacer lo mismo.

Para la letra *Nn*

Escriba la letra *n* en mayúscula y en minúscula, y pida a su niño o niña que identifique las letras. Diga: "Tengo nueve nueces. *Nueve* y *nueces* comienzan con el sonido de la letra *n*". Juntos nombren palabras que comiencen con la letra *n*.

Libros relacionados al tema que pueden leer juntos

Katy No-Pocket *por Emmy Payne. Houghton 1944 (32p)* Katy Canguro no tiene bolsa y busca una para poder cargar a su cangurito Freddy. Disponible en español con el título *Katy no tiene bolsa*.

Lots of Dads *por Shelley Rotner. Dial 1997 (32p)* Las fotos en este libro muestran padres e hijos en actividades variadas, incluyendo trabajo y juego.

Peter's Chair *por Ezra Jack Keats. Harper 1967 (32p) disponible como libro de bolsillo* Peter aprende a aceptar e incluso a querer a su hermanita recién nacida. Disponible en español con el título *La silla de Pedro*.

Buzz *por Janet S. Wong. Harcourt 2000 (32p)* Una mañana muy activa para un niño y sus padres comienza con la alarma del despertador.

A Birthday Basket for Tia *por Pat Mora. Simon 1992 (32p) disponible como libro de bolsillo* Cecilia prepara un regalo especial en honor del cumpleaños de su tía abuela. Disponible en español con el título *Una canasta de cumpleaños para Tía*.

On Mother's Lap *por Ann Herbert Scott. Clarion 1992 (32p) disponible como libro de bolsillo* Un niño inuit descubre que en la falda de su mamá hay espacio para él y para su hermanita.

Theme 3

Name _____   Date _____

	Beginning	Developing	Proficient
Listening Comprehension • Participates in shared and choral reading			
• Listens to a story attentively			
Phonemic Awareness • Can identify beginning sounds			
Phonics • Can recognize initial sounds for *t, b, n*			
Concepts of Print • Recognizes the use of capital at the beginning of a sentence			
• Understands directionality: return sweep			
• Can identify end punctuation			
Reading • Can read wordless stories			
• Can read the high-frequency words *my, like*			
Comprehension • Identifies story structure: character/setting			
• Makes inferences: drawing conclusions			
Writing and Language • Can write simple words			
• Can participate in shared and interactive writing			

For each child, write check marks or notes in the appropriate columns.

Rebus pictures for sentence building

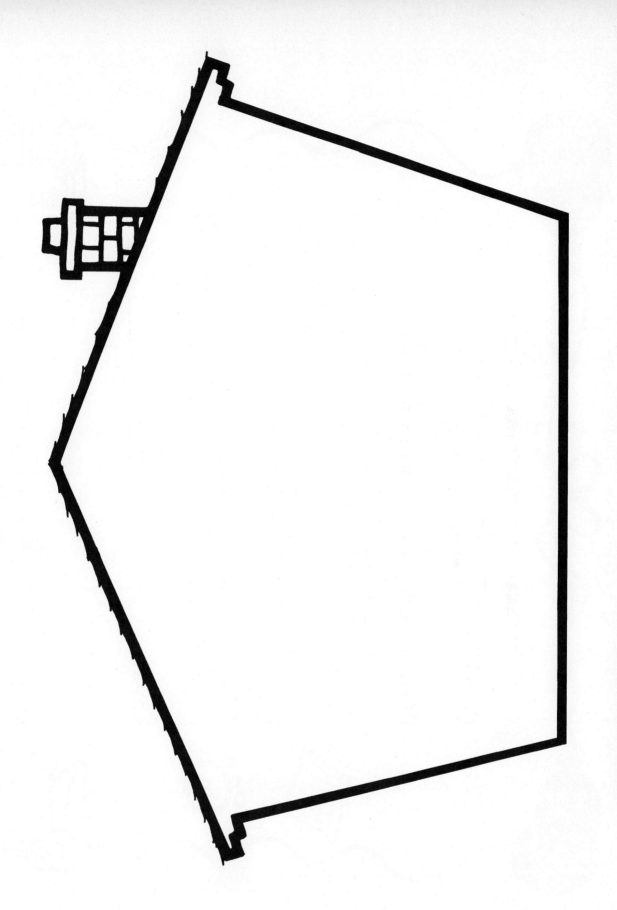

Dear _____ ,

Please come to our Family Breakfast.

When: _____

Time: _____

Love, _____

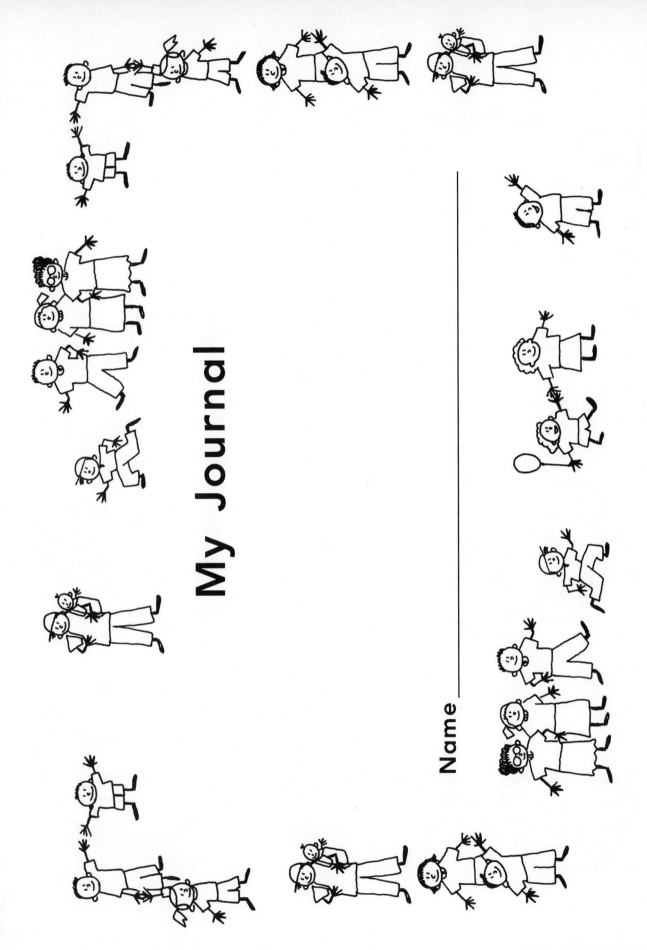

My Journal

Name

Story retelling props for *Goldilocks and the Three Bears*

Story retelling props for *Goldilocks and the Three Bears*

Winter	Summer

Story Retelling props for *The Amazing Little Porridge Pot*

Name: _____

_____

- -

I like _____.

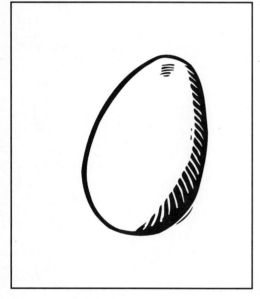

I can write my name!

Name: _____

Date: _____

Newsletter

Friends Together

Dear Family,

Our next reading theme will be *Friends Together*. Kindergarten friends and animal friends are featured in our stories. Children will identify and write the letters *h*, *v*, and *c* and learn the sounds they represent.

Theme-related Activities to Do Together

For the letters *Hh*

Print capital and lower case *h* and have your child identify them. Draw a hat. Have your child name the picture, and say which letter stands for the sound that begins the word *hat*. Then together think of three other things that begin with *h*.

For the letters *Vv*

Form the letter *v* with two pencils and have your child identify the letter. Print capital and lower case *v*. After your child names the letter, say, "I will name two words. One begins with the sound *v* stands for. Is it *car* or *van*; *guitar* or *violin*?"

For the letters *Cc*

Print capital and lower case *c* and have your child identify the letters. Have your child look through grocery store circulars and identify pictures of things whose names begin with the sound the letter *c* stands for — *c* as in *corn*.

Theme-related Books to Enjoy Together!

The Very Lonely Firefly *by Eric Carle. Putnam 1995 (28p)* A firefly flits through a summer night in search of friends.

Bein' With You This Way *by W. Nikola-Lisa. Lee & Low 1995 (32p) also paper* A girl rounds up a group of friends for fun in the park. Available in Spanish as *La alegría de ser tú y yo*.

Two Girls Can *by Keiko Narahashi. McElderry 2000 (32p)* Two girls celebrate all the things that friends can do together.

A Letter to Amy *by Ezra Jack Keats. Harper 1968 (32p) also paper* Peter rushes out in a thunderstorm to send his friend Amy an invitation to his party.

Friend Frog *by Alma Flor Ada. Harcourt 2000 (32p)* Field Mouse can't jump or swim like the frog he meets at the pond, but they become friends.

May I Bring a Friend? *by Beatrice Schenk deRegniers. Macmillan 1964 (32p) also paper* A boy invited to tea with the king and queen takes along his animal friends.

Boletín

Somos amigos

Estimada familia:

El tema de nuestra próxima lectura es *Somos amigos*. En estas historias hay amigos de kindergarten y amigos animales. Los niños aprenderán a identificar y escribir las letras *h, v* y *c* y a identificar los sonidos que representan esas letras.

Actividades para hacer juntos

Para la letra *Hh*

Escriba la letra *h* en mayúscula y en minúscula, y pida a su niño o niña que las identifique. Dibuje un *hongo*. Luego pídale que diga lo que es y que se fije en que la letra inicial *h* no se pronuncia en español. Juntos, piensen en otras tres cosas que comiencen con la letra *h*.

Para la letra *Vv*

Con dos lápices, forme la letra *v* y pida a su niño o niña que la identifique. Escriba la letra *v* en mayúscula y en minúscula. Después de que su niño o niña lea la letra, diga: "Voy a decir dos palabras. Una de ellas comienza con la *v*. ¿Es *venado* o *foco*?, ¿*piano* o *violín*?".

Para la letra *Cc*

Escriba la letra *c* en mayúscula y en minúscula, y pida a su niño o niña que identifique las letras. Luego pídale que vea boletines del supermercado y que identifique ilustraciones de cosas con nombres que comiencen con la letra *c*, como *caja*.

Libros relacionados al tema que pueden leer juntos

The Very Lonely Firefly *por Eric Carle. Putnam 1995 (28p)* Una luciérnaga vuela durante una noche de verano en busca de amigos.

Bein' With You This Way *por W. Nikola-Lisa. Lee & Low 1995 (32p) disponible como libro de bolsillo* Una niña se reúne con un grupo de amigos para ir a divertirse al parque. Disponible en español con el título *La alegría de ser tú y yo.*

Two Girls Can *por Keiko Narahashi. McElderry 2000 (32p)* Dos niñas celebran todo lo que los amigos pueden hacer juntos.

A Letter to Amy *por Ezra Jack Keats. Harper 1968 (32p) disponible como libro de bolsillo* Peter sale durante una tormenta para enviarle a su amiga Amy una invitación a su fiesta.

Friend Frog *por Alma Flor Ada. Harcourt 2000 (32p)* A pesar de que el ratoncito Field Mouse no puede saltar ni nadar como la rana que encuentra en la charca, se hacen amigos.

May I Bring a Friend? *por Beatrice Schenk deRegniers. Macmillan 1964 (32p) disponible como libro de bolsillo* Un niño, que ha sido invitado a tomar té con el rey y la reina, llega con sus amigos animales.

Theme 4

Name _____ Date _____

	Beginning	Developing	Proficient
Listening Comprehension • Participates in shared and choral reading			
• Listens to story attentively			
Phonemic Awareness • Can blend onsets and rimes			
• Can identify words in oral sentences			
Phonics • Can recognize initial sounds for *h, v, c*			
• Can build words with word family -at			
Concepts of Print • Recognizes spaces between words; first letter in a written word			
• Matches speech to print			
Reading • Can read simple decodable texts			
• Can read the high-frequency words *a, to*			
Comprehension • Recognizes organization; can summarize a familiar text			
• Understands cause and effect			
Writing and Language • Can write simple phrases or sentences			
• Can participate in shared and interactive writing			

For each child, write check marks or notes in the appropriate columns.

Rebus pictures for sentence building

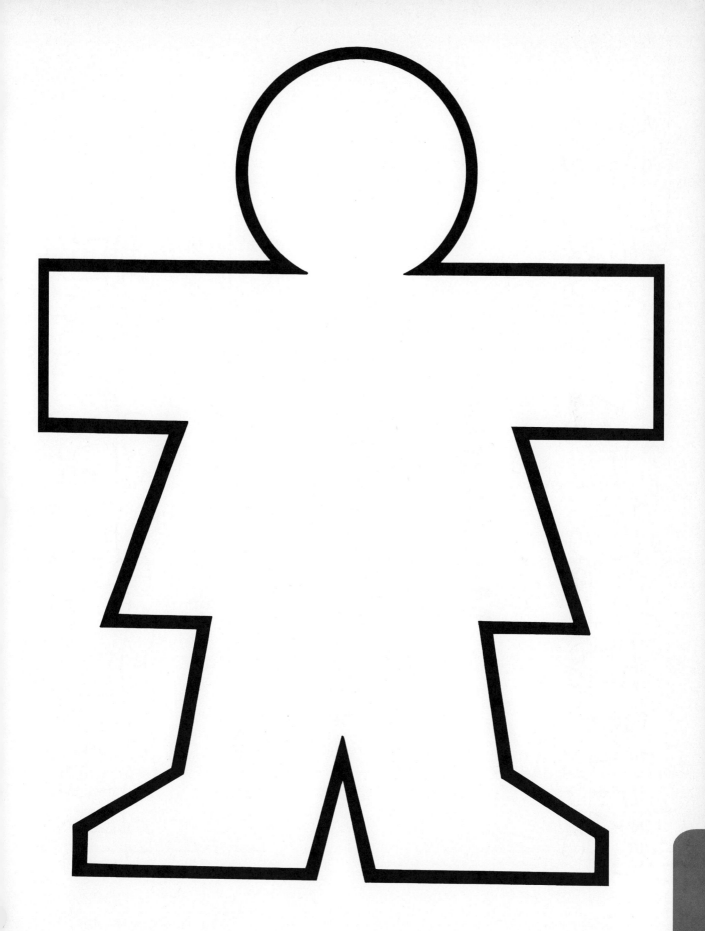

My Journal

Name _____

Rebus pictures for sentence building — nouns

Rebus pictures for sentence building — nouns

Story retelling props for *The Lion and the Mouse*

Story retelling props for *The Lion and the Mouse*

Rebus pictures for sentence building — verbs

Pictures for sorting and classifying

Pictures for sorting and classifying

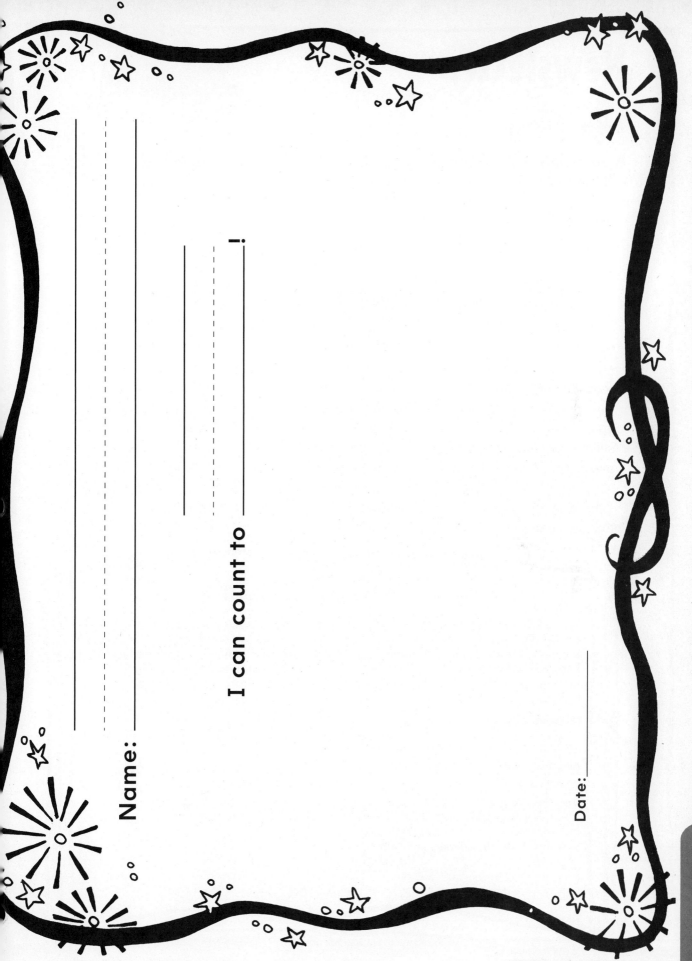

Name:

I can count to ___!

Date: ___

Newsletter

Dear Family,

In our reading theme *Let's Count!*, all the stories children will hear are about counting. Children will also focus on recognizing and writing capital and lower case forms of the letters *p*, *g*, and *f* and learn the sounds they represent.

Theme-Related Activities to Do Together

The letters *Pp*

Shape the letter *p* with a piece of string and have your child identify it. After you print both capital and lower case *p*, ask your child to identify them. Say a word that begins with the sound *p* stands for, and then together name words that begin with *p*.

The letters *Gg*

Print a capital and lower case *g*, and ask your child to name the letters. Say, "Gail has a goat. The words *Gail* and *goat* begin with the sound the letter *g* stands for." Help your child name other words that begin with *g*.

The letters *Ff*

Print both capital and lower case *f* and have your child identify the letters. Say, "I'm going to say two words that begin with the sound the letter *f* stands for: *funny fish*." Take turns saying other words that begin with *f*.

Theme-Related Books to Enjoy Together!

Three Friends/Tres Amigos *by Maria Cristina Brusca. Holt 1995 (32p)* Three friends—a cowboy, a cowgirl, and their horse—count their way through adventures in the southwest. Text in English and Spanish.

Millions of Cats *by Wanda Gag. McCann 1928 (32p) also paper* An old man who sets off to find one kitten returns home with millions of cats. Available in Spanish as *Millones de gatos.*

Can You Count Ten Toes? *by Lezlie Evans. Houghton 1999 (32p)* Children are invited to count to ten in languages including Spanish, Korean, and Zulu.

Five Little Ducks *by Pamela Paparone. North-South 1995 (32p) also paper* Mother duck sets out to find her disappearing ducklings in this traditional rhyme. Available in Spanish as *Los cinco patitos.*

Let's Count *by Tana Hoban. Greenwillow 1999 (32p)* Photographs of everyday objects introduce the numbers from one to one hundred.

Somewhere in the Ocean *by Jennifer Ward and T. J. Marsh. Rising Moon 2000 (32p)* This counting song presents sea animals and their offspring.

Boletín

Estimada familia:

En el tema *Vamos a contar*, todas las historias que los niños van a oír son para contar. Los niños van a aprender a reconocer y a escribir las letras mayúsculas y minúsculas para *p*, *g* y *f* y a identificar los sonidos que representan esas letras.

¡Vamos a contar!

Actividades para hacer juntos

La letra *Pp*

Forme la letra *p* con un cordel y pida a su niño o niña que identifique la letra. Después de que escriba la *p* en mayúscula y en minúscula, pídale que las identifique. Diga una palabra que comience con el sonido de la letra *p*, y luego ambos digan palabras con la letra *p* inicial.

La letra *Gg*

Escriba la letra *g* en mayúscula y en minúscula, y pida a su niño o niña que identifique las letras. Diga: "Gabriel tiene una gallina. Las palabras *Gabriel* y *gallina* comienzan con el sonido de la letra *g*". Ayude a su niño o niña a nombrar otras palabras con la letra *g* inicial.

La letra *Ff*

Escriba la letra *f* en mayúscula y en minúscula, y pida a su niño o niña que las identifique. Diga: "Voy a decir dos palabras que comienzan con el sonido de la letra *f*: *fin feliz*". Tomen turnos para decir otras palabras con la letra *f* incial.

Libros relacionados al tema que pueden leer juntos

Three Friends/Tres Amigos *por María Cristina Brusca. Holt 1995 (32p)* A tres amigos les gusta contar durante sus aventuras en el suroeste de los Estados Unidos. El texto del libro aparece en inglés y en español.

Millions of Cats *por Wanda Gag. McCann 1928 (32p) disponible como libro de bolsillo* Un viejito que va en busca de un gatito regresa a casa con millones de gatos. Disponible en español con el título *Millones de gatos.*

Can You Count Ten Toes? *por Lezlie Evans. Houghton 1999 (32p)* Los niños pueden contar hasta diez en varios idiomas que incluyen español, inglés, coreano y zulu.

Five Little Ducks *por Pamela Paparone. North-South 1995 (32p) disponible como libro de bolsillo* En esta rima tradicional, la mamá pata va en busca de sus patitos perdidos. Disponible en español con el título *Los cinco patitos.*

Let's Count *por Tana Hoban. Greenwillow 1999 (32p)* Fotos de objetos comunes presentan los números del uno al cien.

Somewhere in the Ocean *por Jennifer Ward y T. J. Marsh. Rising Moon 2000 (32p)* Esta canción de contar presenta animales marinos y sus crías.

Theme 5

Name _____   Date _____

	Beginning	Developing	Proficient
Listening Comprehension • Participates in shared and choral reading			
• Listens to story attentively			
Phonemic Awareness • Can blend onsets and rimes			
• Can identify words in oral sentences			
Phonics • Can recognize initial sounds *p, g,* and *f*			
• Can build words with word family *-an*			
Concepts of Print • Distinguishes between letter, word, and sentence			
• Recognizes first/last letter in a written word			
Reading • Can read simple decodable texts			
• Can read the high-frequency words *and, go*			
Comprehension • Understands how to categorize and classify			
• Recognizes story structure: beginning, middle, end			
Writing and Language • Can write simple phrases or sentences			
• Can participate in shared and interactive writing			

For each child, write check marks or notes in the appropriate columns.

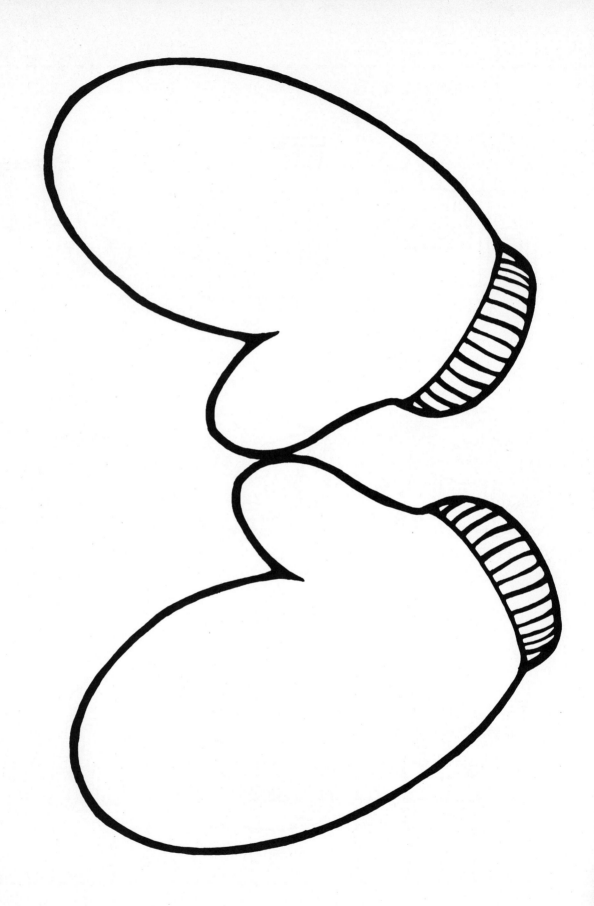

My Journal

Name: _____

Name: _____

3

Name: _____

4

Name: _____

5

Name: _____

6

7

Name: _____

8

9

Name: _____

10	

Name:

I can say my ABC's.

Date:

Newsletter

Dear Family,

For the next few weeks, our kindergarten reading theme will be *Sunshine and Raindrops*, a theme about weather. Children will learn to recognize and write capital and lower case forms of the letters *l*, *k*, and *qu*, and identify the sounds these letters represent.

Sunshine and Raindrops

Theme-Related Activities to Do Together

The letters *Ll*

Print capital *L* and lower case *l* and have your child identify the letters. Say, "Lynn is a name that begins with the sound the letter *l* stands for." Help your child think of other names that begin with *l*.

The letters *Kk*

Print both capital and lower case *k*, and ask your child to identify them. As you, kick your leg, say "kick" and name another word that begins with the *k* sound. Take turns saying other words that begin with *k*.

The Letters *Qu, qu*

As you print *Qu* and *qu*, tell your child that the letter *q* has a partner letter, *u*. Ask your child to name the letters. Then say, "The queen likes quail. *Queen* and *quail* begin with the sound the letters *qu* stand for." Help your child name other words that begin with *qu*.

Theme-Related Books to Enjoy Together!

The Snowy Day by *Ezra Jack Keats. Viking 1962 (32p) also paper* A small boy discovers the joys of a snowy day. Available in Spanish as *Un día de nieve.*

A Year for Kiko by *Ferida Wolff. Houghton 1977 (32p)* Throughout the seasons, Kiko enjoys activities from catching snowflakes to cooling off in a pool.

Katy and the Big Snow by *Virginia Lee Burton. Houghton 1943 (40p) also paper* Katy the snowplow saves the day when a winter storm threatens to shut down the city of Geopolis.

Bringing the Rain to Kapiti Plain by *Verna Aardema. Dial 1981 (32p) also paper* In a cumulative African tale, Ki-pat brings rain to the drought-stricken Kapiti Plain.

Rain Song by *Lezlie Evans. Houghton 1995 (32p) also paper* Poetic text celebrates the excitement of a summer thunderstorm.

Weather by *Lee Bennett Hopkins. Harper 1994 (64p) also paper* A collection of short, rhyming poems about all kinds of weather.

Boletín

Sol y nubes

Estimada familia:

Durante las próximas semanas, nuestra clase de kindergarten leerá el tema acerca del tiempo *Sol y nubes*. Los niños van a aprender a reconocer las formas máyuscula y minúscula y los sonidos de las letras *l* y *k*, y la combinación de letras *qu*.

Actividades para hacer juntos

La letra *Ll*

Escriba la letra mayúscula *L* y la letra minúscula *l*, y pida a su niño o niña que las identifique. Diga: "Lynn es un nombre que comienza con el sonido de la letra *l*". Ayude a su niño o niña a pensar en otras cosa que comiencen con la letra *l*.

La letra *Kk*

Escriba la letra *k* en mayúscula y en minúscula, y pida a su niño o niña que identifique las letras. Mientras dibuja un kiosko para su niño o niña, nombre otra palabra que comience con la letra *k*. Túrnense para decir otras palabras que comiencen con la letra *k*.

La combinación de letras *Qu qu*

Explique a su niño o niña que la letra *q* siempre tiene una compañera, la letra *u*. Luego diga: "*Quiero* y *queso* comienzan con la combinacion de letras *qu*". Ayude a su niño o niña a nombrar otras palabras que comiencen con *qu*.

Libros relacionados al tema que pueden leer juntos

The Snowy Day *por Ezra Jack Keats. Viking 1962 (32p) disponible como libro de bolsillo* Un niño descubre lo divertido que es un día de nieve. Disponible en español con el título *Un día de nieve*.

A Year for Kiko *por Ferida Wolff. Houghton 1977 (32p)* Kiko disfruta de actividades en las distintas estaciones del año, de jugar con copos de nieve a refrescarse en la alberca para protegerse del calor.

Katy and the Big Snow *por Virginia Lee Burton. Houghton 1943 (40p) disponible como libro de bolsillo* Cuando una tormenta invernal amenaza con paralizar la ciudad de Geópolis, Katy, la quitanieve, soluciona el problema.

Bringing the Rain to Kapiti Plain *por Verna Aardema. Dial 1981 (32p) disponible como libro de bolsillo* En un cuento africano, Ki-pat trae lluvia a la seca llanura de Kapiti.

Rain Song *por Lezlie Evans. Houghton 1995 (32p) disponible como libro de bolsillo* Texto poético que celebra lo emocionante que puede ser una tormenta de verano.

Weather *por Lee Bennett Hopkins. Harper 1994 (64p) disponible como libro de bolsillo* Una colección de poemas cortos en rima acerca de variadas condiciones del tiempo.

Theme 6

Name _____   Date _____

	Beginning	Developing	Proficient
Listening Comprehension • Participates in shared and choral reading			
• Listens to a story attentively			
Phonemic Awareness • Blends onsets and rimes			
• Segments onsets and rimes			
Phonics • Recognizes sounds for consonants *k, l, qu*			
• Builds words with word family *-it*			
Concepts of Print • Uses a capital at the beginning of a sentence			
• Uses end punctuation (period, question mark, exclamation mark)			
• Understands quotation marks			
Reading • Reads simple decodable texts			
• Reads the high-frequency words *is, here*			
Comprehension • Distinguishes fantasy from realism			
• Recognizes elements of plot (problem, solution)			
Writing and Language • Writes simple phrases			
• Participates in shared and interactive writing			

For each child, write check marks or notes in the appropriate columns.

Rebus pictures for sentence building

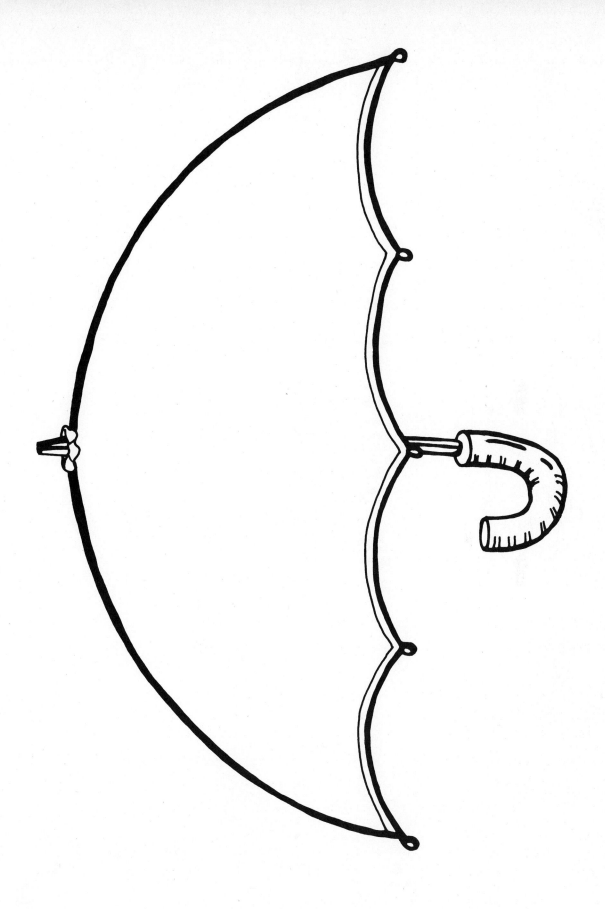

My Journal

Name

Story retelling props for *The Woodcutter's Cap*

Story retelling props for *The Woodcutter's Cap*

I learned a new letter today!

Name: _____

Here it is _____.

Date: _____

Newsletter

Wheels Go Around

Dear Family,

Wheels Go Around is our next reading theme. The Read Aloud and Big Book stories children will enjoy are about wheels and transportation. Children will learn to recognize and write the letters *d* and *z* and identify the sounds they represent.

Theme-Related Activities to Do Together

The letters *Dd*

Print both capital and lower case *d* and ask your child to identify them. Draw a drum. Have your child name the picture, and then tell which letter stands for the beginning sound of the word *drum*. Together think of other words beginning with *d*.

The letters *Zz*

Form the letter *z* with three sticks and have your child identify the letter. Print capital and lower case *z*, and have your child identify them. Say, "I will say two words. One begins with the sound *z* stands for. Is it *park* or *zoo*; *button* or *zipper*?"

Counting 1 to 10

Play Counting 1 to 10. One player names a category and begins counting items within the category from 1 to 10. For example, "1 hat, 2 hats, . . ." When a player taps the other player on the shoulder, she or he continues the count.

Theme-Related Books to Enjoy Together!

Mike Mulligan and His Steam Shovel *by Virginia Lee Burton. Houghton 1939 (48p) also paper* Mike and his steam shovel, Mary Anne, don't give up when they lose their job. Available in Spanish as *Mike Mulligan y su máquina maravillosa.*

Curious George Rides a Bike *by H.A. Rey. Houghton 1952 (48p) also paper* Curious George gets into all sorts of trouble helping a boy with his paper route.

The Little Engine That Could *by Watty Piper. Putnam 1930 (48p) also paper* A small but determined train engine helps get food and toys to children waiting in a valley. Available in Spanish as *La pequeña locomotora que sí pudo.*

Seymour Simon's Book of Trucks *by Seymour Simon. Harper 2000 (32p)* Large photos of different kinds of trucks accompany descriptions of the jobs they do.

Night at the Fair *by Donald Crews. Greenwillow 1998 (32p)* Nighttime is a great time to be at the fair, and the best ride of all at the fair is the giant ferris wheel.

Sheep in a Jeep *by Nancy Shaw. Houghton 1986 (32p)* Lively rhyming verse tells how five sheep out for a ride in their jeep run into trouble.

Boletín

Estimada familia:

Ruedan y ruedan es nuestro tema siguiente. Las historias de lectura en voz alta (Read Aloud stories) y Los libros grandes (Big Books) que los niños leerán se tratan de las ruedas y del transporte. Los niños aprenderán a reconocer y a leer las letras *d* y *z*, y a identificar esas letras y sus sonidos.

Ruedan y ruedan

Actividades para hacer juntos

La letra *Dd*

Escriba la letra *d* en mayúscula y en minúscula, y pida a su niño o niña que las identifique. Dibuje un diente. Pida a su niño o niña que identifique el dibujo, y que diga la letra inicial de la palabra *diente*.

La letra *Zz*

Escriba la letra *z* en mayúscula y en minúscula, y pida a su niño o niña que las identifique. Diga: "Voy a decir dos palabras. Una comienza con el sonido de la letra *z*. ¿Es la palabra *parque* o *zoológico*? ¿Es la palabra *mapache* o *zorrillo*?".

Contar de 1 a 10

Jueguen a contar de 1 a 10. Un jugador nombra una categoría y comienza a contar objetos en esa categoría de 1 a 10. Por ejemplo: "1 sombrero, 2 sombreros, …". Cuando un jugador toca el hombro de otro jugador, el otro jugador continúa contando.

Libros relacionados al tema que pueden leer juntos

Mike Mulligan and His Steam Shovel *por Virginia Lee Burton. Houghton 1939 (48p) disponible como libro de bolsillo* Mike y su pala de vapor, Mary Anne, no se dan por vencidos cuando pierden sus trabajos. Disponible en español con el título *Mike Mulligan y su máquina maravillosa*.

Curious George Rides a Bike *por H. A. Rey. Houghton 1952 (48p) disponible como libro de bolsillo* Jorge Curioso se mete en toda clase de problemas cuando trata de ayudar a un niño que reparte periódicos.

The Little Engine That Could *por Watty Piper. Putnam 1930 (48p) disponible como libro de bolsillo* Una pequeña pero determinada locomotora ayuda a obtener comida y juguetes para los niños que esperan en el valle. Disponible en español con el título *La pequeña locomotora que sí pudo*.

Seymour Simon's Book of Trucks *por Seymour Simon. Harper 2000 (32p)* Fotos grandes de distintos tipos de camiones acompañan las descripciones de los trabajos que hace cada uno.

Night at the Fair *por Donald Crews. Greenwillow 1998 (32p)* Cuando es de noche, es la mejor hora para ir a la feria, y la mejor atracción es poder montar en la gran rueda gigante.

Sheep in a Jeep *por Nancy Shaw. Houghton 1986 (32p)* Este animado verso en rima describe cómo se metieron en problemas cinco ovejas cuando fueron a dar una vuelta en su jeep.

Theme 7

Name _____   Date _____

	Beginning	Developing	Proficient
Listening Comprehension • Participates in shared and choral reading			
• Listens to a story attentively			
Phonemic Awareness • Blends phonemes			
• Identifies beginning sound			
Phonics • Recognizes sounds for consonants *d, z*			
• Builds words with word family *-ig*			
Concepts of Print • Uses capital at the beginning of a sentence			
• Uses end punctuation (period, question mark)			
Reading • Reads simple decodable texts			
• Reads the high-frequency words *for, have*			
Comprehension • Recognizes text organization; can summarize			
• Understands cause and effect			
• Makes inferences, predictions			
Writing and Language • Writes simple phrases or sentences			
• Participates in shared and interactive writing			

For each child, write check marks or notes in the appropriate columns.

Rebus pictures for sentence building

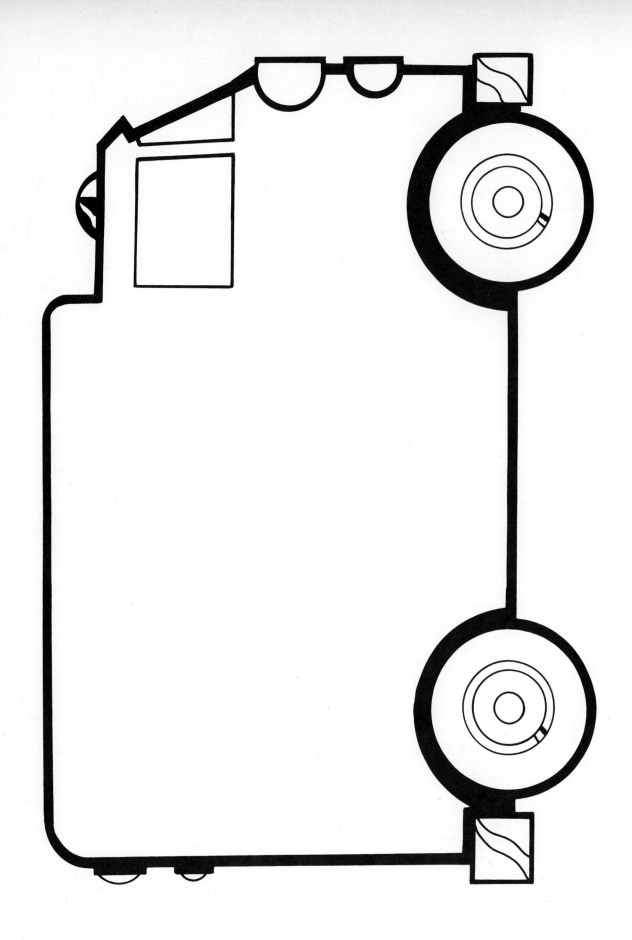

Shape Paper for The Writing Center

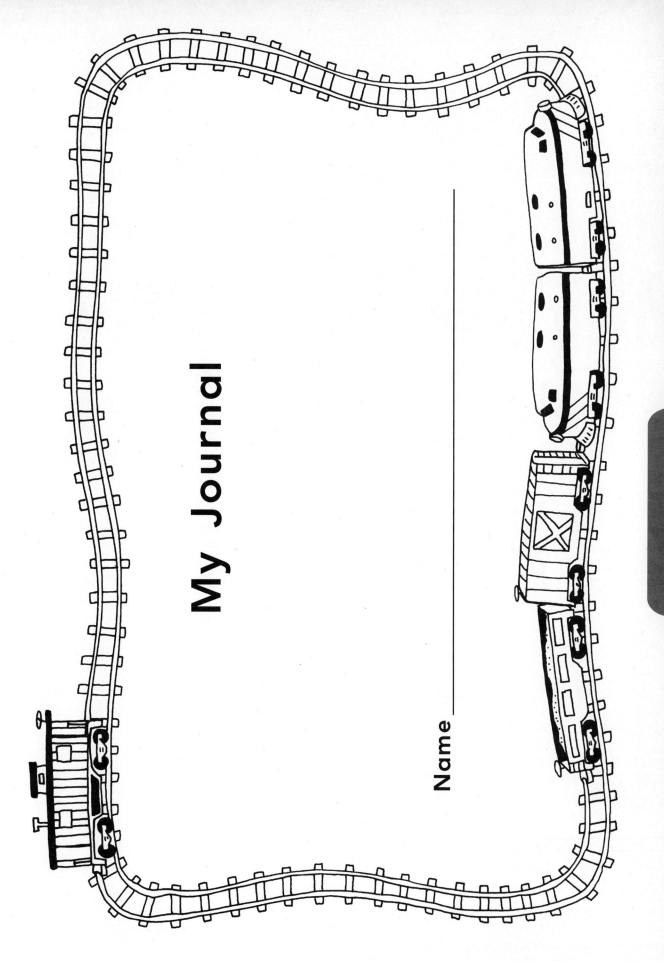

My Journal

Name _____

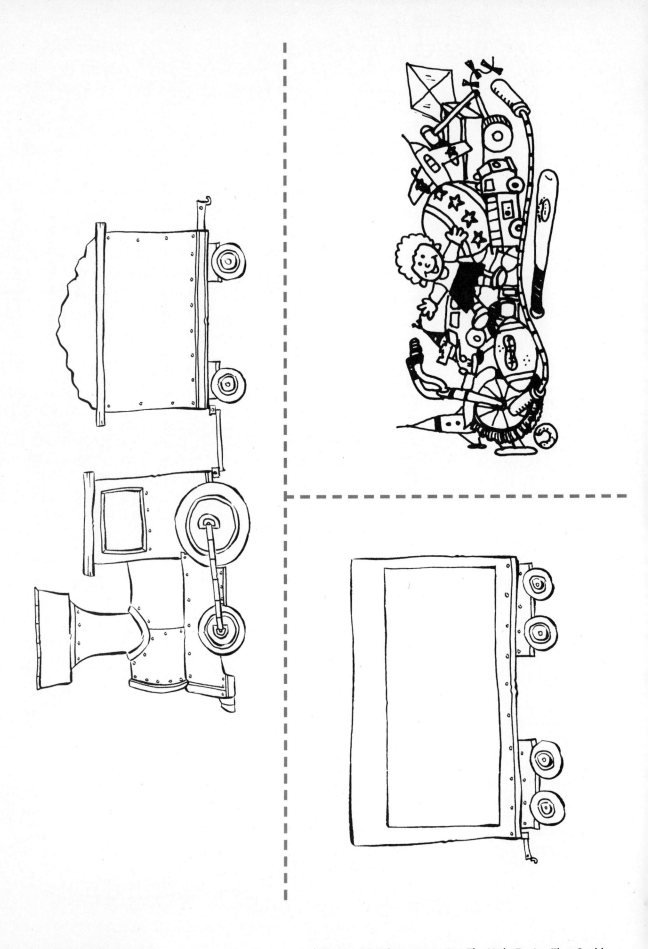

Story retelling props for *The Little Engine That Could*

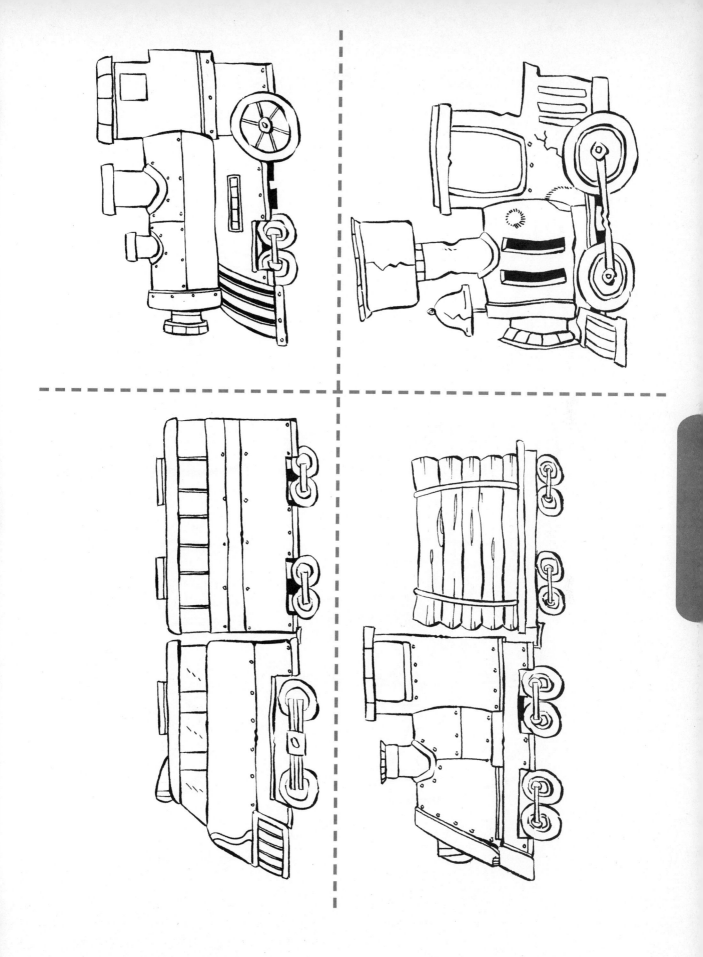

Story retelling props for *The Little Engine That Could*

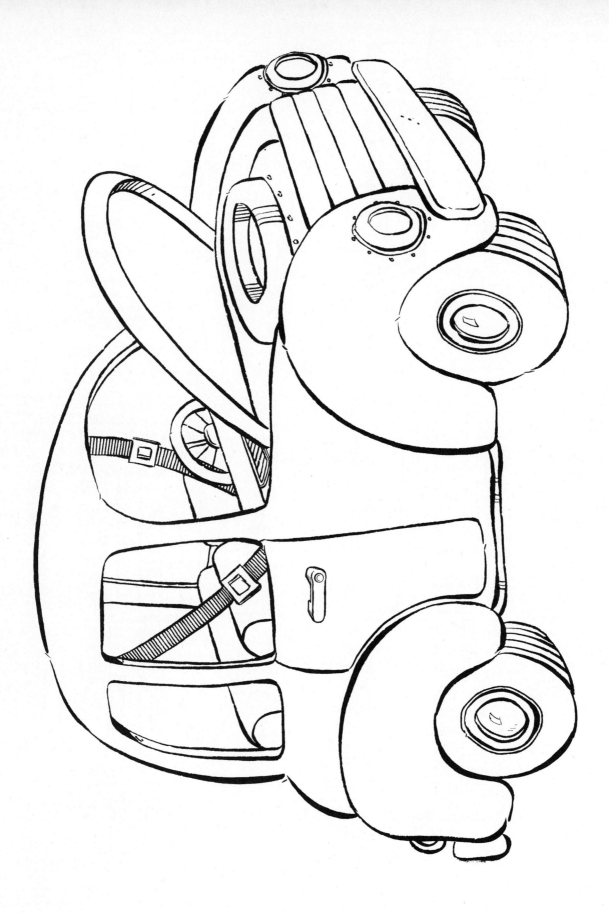

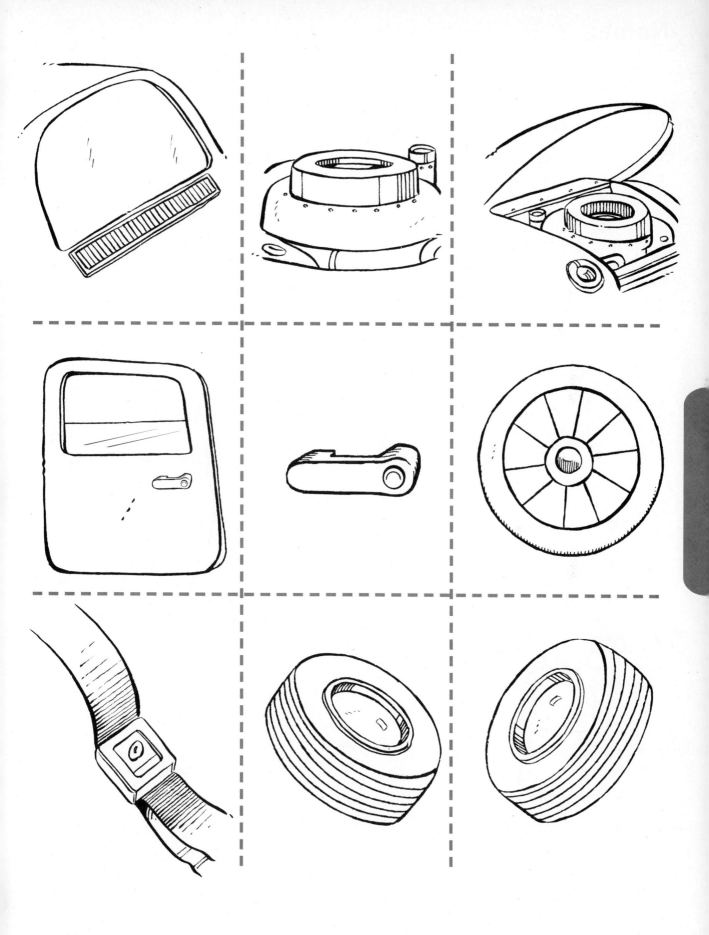

Parts of a Car

Name: _____

Story retelling props for *Mr. Gumpy's Motor Car*

Name: _____

Name:

Good Job!

Date:

Newsletter

Down on the Farm

Dear Family,

Our next reading theme will be *Down on the Farm*. Besides enjoying the stories from the country, children will learn to recognize and write capital and lower case forms of the letter *x*, as well as learn about the sound it represents.

Theme-Related Activities to Do Together

The Letters *Xx*

Print both capital and lower case *x*. and have your child identify the letters. Then slowly say: *ox*, *ax*, and *box*. Tell children that *x* stands for the sound at the end of the words *ox*, *ax*, and *box*. Help your child name other words ending with *x*.

Find the Color

Name a color pictured in a grocery circular, and have your child point to an item that is that color. Focus on colors such as red, orange, yellow, green, blue, and purple.

Let's Count

Taking turns, play a counting game. One player names a building such as a farmhouse. The other player then names different items (from 1 to 10) that might be in the building. For example, "1 stove, 2 windows, 3 cats . . ."

Theme-Related Books to Enjoy Together!

Rosie's Walk *by Pat Hutchins. Simon 1968 (32p)* A hungry fox slinks behind an unsuspecting hen as she walks around the barnyard. Available in Spanish as *El paseo de Rosie.*

Big Red Barn *by Margaret Wise Brown. Harper 1989 (32p) also paper* Rhyming text tells the story of the animals that live in a big red barn. Available in Spanish as *El gran granero rojo.*

A Day at Greenhill Farm *by Sue Nicholson. DK 1998 (32p) also paper* When the rooster crows, a busy day begins at Greenhill Farm.

No, No Titus! *by Claire Masurel. North-South 1997 (32p) also paper* When a fox tries to raid a chicken coop, a farm dog finally discovers his job. Available in Spanish as *¡No, Tito, No!*

This and That *by Julie Sykes. Holt 1996 (32p)* Cat collects "this and that" from her farmyard friends to make a bed for her new kittens.

Old MacDonald Had a Farm *by Carol Jones. Houghton 1989 (32p) also paper* A familiar song becomes a game as readers look through a peephole for each animal.

Boletín

En la granja

Estimada familia:

Nuestro próximo tema es *En la granja*. Además de disfrutar las historias del campo, los niños aprenden a reconocer y a escribir la letra *x* en mayúscula y en minúscula y a identificar el sonido que representa esa letra.

Actividades para hacer juntos

La letra *Xx*

Escriba la letra *x* en mayúscula y en minúscula. Luego diga *oxígeno* y *taxi*. Diga a los niños que identifiquen el sonido que representa la letra *x* en las palabras *oxígeno* y *taxi*. Ayude a su niño o niña a nombrar otras palabras con la letra *x*.

Busquen el color

Nombre un color que aparezca en un boletín del supermercado, y pida a su niño o niña que señale un objeto que sea del mismo color. Escoja colores como el rojo, anaranjado, amarillo, verde, azul y morado.

Contemos

Túrnense para jugar un juego de contar. Un jugador nombra un tipo de edificio, como una granja. Luego el otro jugador nombra (de 1 a 10) distintas cosas que puede haber en ese tipo de edificio. Por ejemplo: "1 horno, 2 ventanas, 3 gatos …".

Libros relacionados al tema que pueden leer juntos

Rosie's Walk *por Pat Hutchins. Simon 1968 (32p)* Una zorra hambrienta sigue furtivamente a una gallina ingenua que se pasea por su corral. Disponible en español con el título *El paseo de Rosie.*

Big Red Barn *por Margaret Wise Brown. Harper 1989 (32p) disponible como libro de bolsillo* Texto en rima que cuenta la historia de animales que viven en un enorme granero rojo. Disponible en español con el título *El gran granero rojo.*

A Day at Greenhill Farm *por Sue Nicholson. DK 1998 (32p) disponible como libro de bolsillo* Un día agitado comienza tan pronto como el gallo canta en la granja Greenhill Farm.

No, No Titus! *por Claire Masurel. North-South 1997 (32p) disponible como libro de bolsillo* Cuando un zorro intenta atacar el gallinero, un perro de granja por fin descubre cual es su trabajo. Disponible en español con el título *¡No, Tito, No!*

This and That *por Julie Sykes. Holt 1996 (32p)* Un gato recoge "esto y lo otro" de sus amigos en el corral de la granja, para hacer una cama para sus gatitos recién nacidos.

Old MacDonald Had a Farm *por Carol Jones. Houghton 1989 (32p) disponible como libro de bolsillo* Esta conocida canción se convierte en un juego, a medida que los lectores ven a cada animal como si los estuvieran observando a través de una rendija.

Theme 8

Name _____   Date _____

	Beginning	Developing	Proficient
Listening Comprehension • Participates in shared and choral reading			
• Listens to a story attentively			
Phonemic Awareness • Blends phonemes			
• Identifies beginning sounds			
Phonics • Recognizes sound for final *x*			
• Builds words with word family *-ox*			
Concepts of Print • Recognizes use of all capital letters			
• Demonstrates reading direction, return sweep			
Reading • Reads simple decodable texts			
• Reads the high-frequency words *said, the*			
Comprehension • Distinguishes fantasy from realism in text			
• Notes important details			
• Draws conclusions			
Writing and Language • Draws and labels images			
• Writes simple phrases or sentences			
• Participates in shared writing			

For each child, write check marks or notes in the appropriate columns.

Rebus pictures for sentence building

Rebus pictures for sentence building

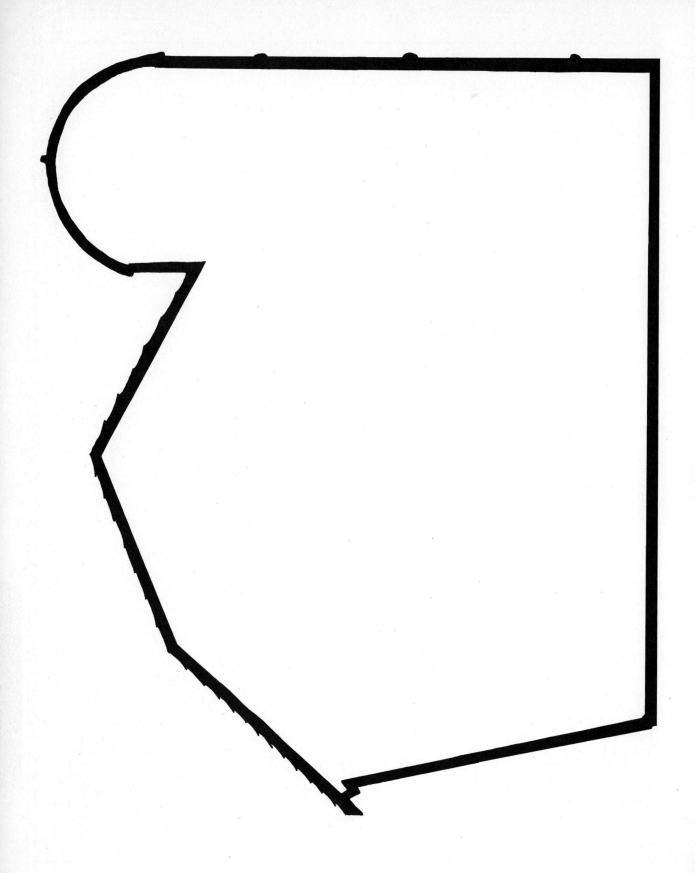

Shape Paper for The Writing Center

My Journal

Name

Story retelling props for *Cows in the Kitchen*

Story retelling props for *Cows in the Kitchen*

Story retelling props for *The Enormous Turnip*

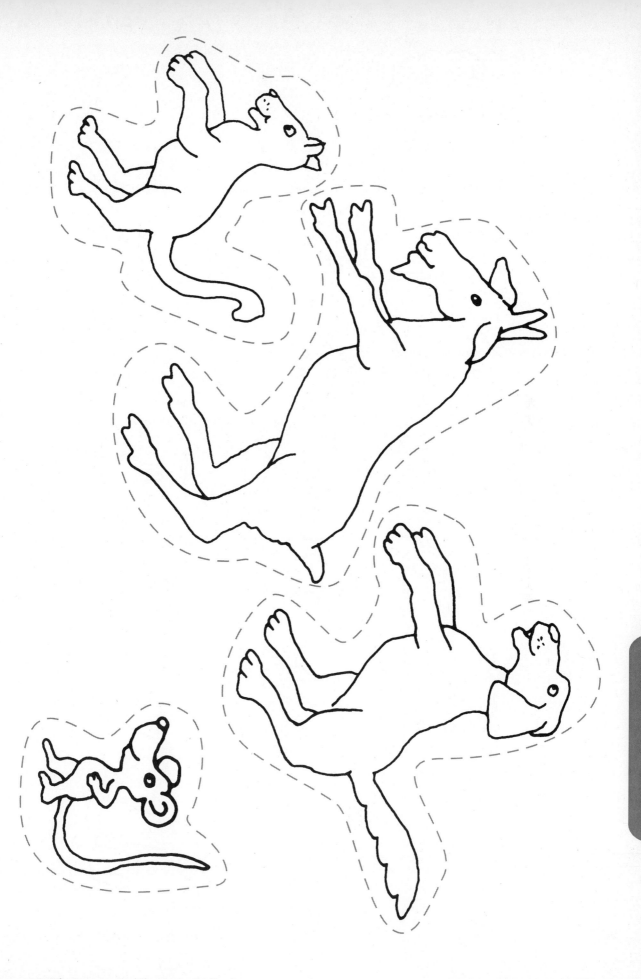

Story retelling props for *The Enormous Turnip*

Story retelling props for *The Enormous Turnip*

Name: _____

I can write some words!

Date: _____

Newsletter

Spring Is Here

Dear Family,

Our next reading theme will be *Spring Is Here*. Our Big Book selections include a contrast of the serious and the silly. Children will work on recognizing and writing the letters *w* and *y* and learn the sounds these letters represent.

Theme-Related Activities to Do Together

The Letters *Ww*

Print capital and lower case *w* and have your child identify them. Draw a window, and have your child name the picture. Then say the letter that stands for the beginning sound of the word *window*, and name other words that begin with *w*.

The Letters *Yy*

Form the letter *y* with three crayons and have your child identify the letter. Print capital and lower case *y*. After your child names the letters, say, "I will say two words. One begins with the sound *y* stands for. Is it *lawn* or *yard*; *blue* or *yellow*?"

Colors

Play the game "I Spy," using objects of different colors. For example, one player says, "I spy something blue." Players take turns guessing each other's clues. Start with the colors green, yellow, orange and purple, and then include color words such as magenta or turquoise.

Theme-Related Books to Enjoy Together!

The Happy Day by Ruth Krauss. *Harper 1949 (32p) also paper* Woodland animals wake from their winter's sleep to discover the first sign of spring. Available in Spanish as *Un día feliz*.

Spring by Karen Bryant-Mole. *Heinemann. 1997 (24p)* Clear text and color photos present everyday things found in spring. Available in Spanish as *Primavera*.

Make Way for Ducklings by Robert McCloskey. *Viking 1941 (68p) also paper* Mrs. Mallard and her ducklings find a safe home in the Boston Public Garden in this Caldecott-Medal winning story. Available in Spanish as *Abran paso a los patitos*.

Hopper Hunts for Spring by Marcus Pfister. *North-South 1992 (32p) also paper* When Hopper the bunny's mother tells him spring is coming, he bounds away to meet what he thinks is a new playmate. Available in Spanish as *Saltarín y la primavera*.

Henry and Mudge in Puddle Trouble by Cynthia Rylant. *Simon 1996 (48p) also paper* Henry and his big dog Mudge share springtime adventures together. Available in Spanish as *Henry y Mudge con barro hasta el rabo*.

Possum and the Peeper by Anne Hunter. *Houghton 1998 (32p)* Roused from his winter nap, Possum sets out to discover what's making the noise that woke him.

Boletín

Estimada familia:

Nuestro próximo tema de lectura es *Llegó la primavera*. Pasajes del libro grande (Big Book) incluyen un contraste entre lo serio y lo divertido. Los niños identifican y escriben las letras *w* e *y*, y aprenden a identificar los sonidos que representan.

Llegó la primavera

Actividades para hacer juntos

La letra *Ww*

Escriba la letra *w* en mayúscula y en minúscula, y pida a su niño o niña que las identifique. Diga las palabras *Washington* y *Wilson*, y diga a su niño o niña que la letra *w* representa el sonido inicial de esas dos palabras.

La letra *Yy*

Escriba la letra *y* en mayúscula y en minúscula. Diga: "Voy a decir dos palabras. Una comienza con el sonido de la letra *y*. ¿Es *camello* o *yegua*? ¿Es *yarda* o *metro*?".

Colores

Jueguen "Veo, veo" con objetos de distintos colores. Por ejemplo, un jugador dice: "Veo, veo algo azul". Cuando el otro jugador adivina el objeto que vio el primer jugador, los jugadores cambian de papel en el juego.

Libros relacionados al tema que pueden leer juntos

The Happy Day *por Ruth Krauss. Harper 1949 (32p) disponible como libro de bolsillo* Animales del bosque despiertan de su sueño invernal y descubren las primeras señales de la primavera. Disponible en español con el título *Un día feliz*.

Spring *por Karen Bryant-Mole. Heinemann. 1997 (24p)* Texto claro y fotos a color presentan objetos comunes que se encuentran en primavera. Disponible en español con el título *Primavera*.

Make Way for Ducklings *por Robert McCloskey. Viking 1941 (68p) disponible como libro de bolsillo* En esta historia premiada con la medalla de Caldecott, la mamá pata y sus patitos hallan un hogar seguro en el jardín público de Boston. Disponible en español con el título *Abran paso a los patitos*.

Hopper Hunts for Spring *por Marcus Pfister. North-South 1992 (32p) disponible como libro de bolsillo* La primavera está por llegar, y Hopper va a encontrarse con lo que piensa que será un nuevo amigo. Disponible en español con el título *Saltarín y la primavera*.

Henry and Mudge in Puddle Trouble *por Cynthia Rylant. Simon 1996 (48p) disponible como libro de bolsillo* Henry y su enorme perro Mudge comparten juntos aventuras durante la primavera. Disponible en español con el título *Henry y Mudge con barro hasta el rabo*.

Possum and the Peeper *por Anne Hunter. Houghton 1998 (32p)* Al ser despertado de su siesta de invierno, una zarigüeya trata de descubrir de dónde viene el ruido que la despertó.

Theme 9

Name _____   Date _____

	Beginning	Developing	Proficient
Listening Comprehension • Participates in shared and choral reading			
• Listens to a story attentively			
Phonemic Awareness • Blends phonemes			
Phonics • Recognizes initial sounds for *w* and *y*			
• Builds words with word families -*et* and -*en*			
Concepts of Print • Distinguishes letter, word, sentence			
• Recognizes first and last letter in a word			
Reading • Reads simple decodable texts			
• Reads the high-frequency words *play, she*			
Comprehension • Determines sequence of events			
• Categorizes and classifies			
• Recognizes characters in a text			
Writing and Language • Writes simple words			
• Writes simple phrases or sentences			
• Enjoys writing independently			

For each child, write check marks or notes in the appropriate columns.

Rebus pictures for sentence building

Shape Paper for The Writing Center

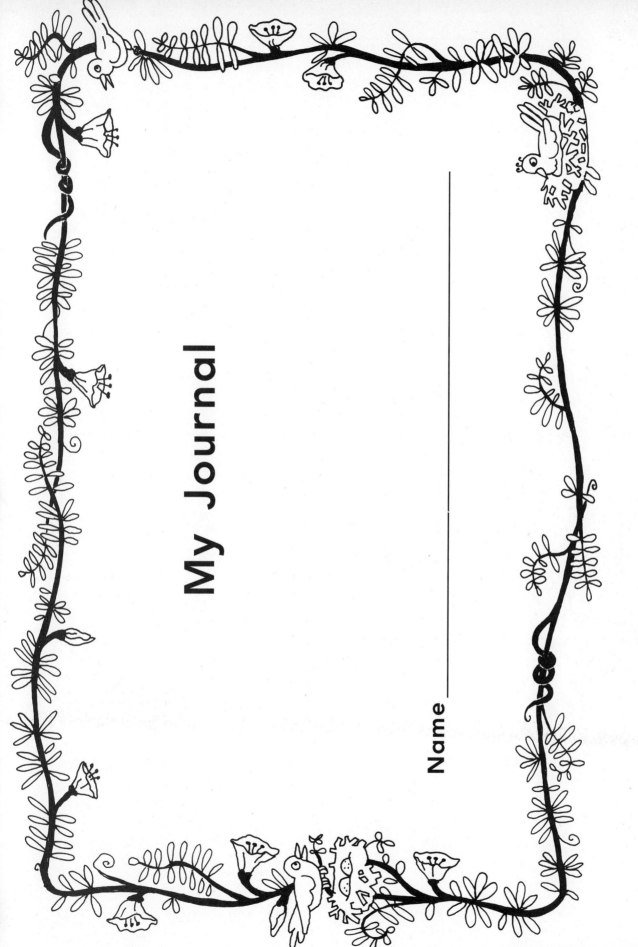

My Journal

Name _____

Name: _____

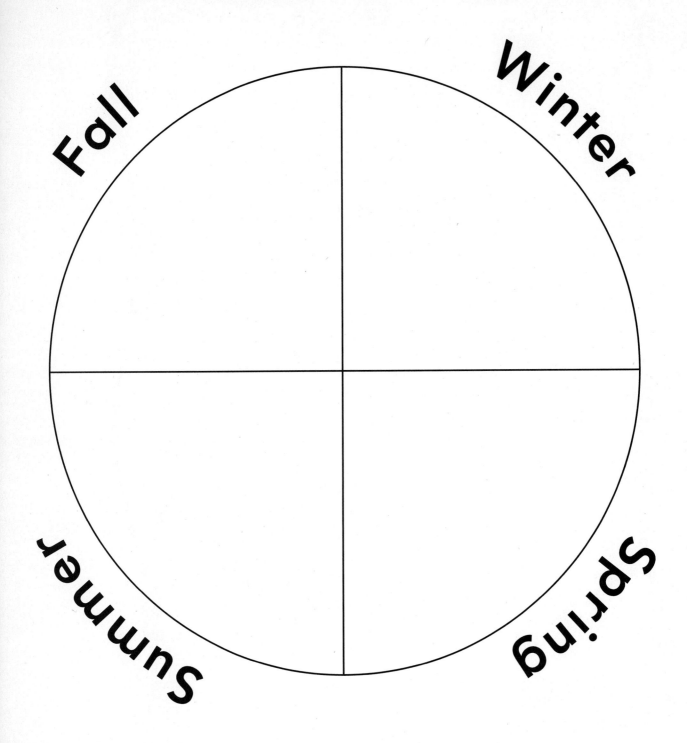

Story retelling props for *The Tortoise and the Hare*

Story retelling props for *The Tortoise and the Hare*

Story retelling props for *The Three Billy Goats Gruff*

Story retelling props for *The Three Billy Goats Gruff*

Story retelling props for *The Three Billy Goats Gruff*

Story retelling props for *Mrs. McNosh Hangs Up Her Wash*

Story retelling props for *Mrs. McNosh Hangs Up Her Wash*

Name: _____

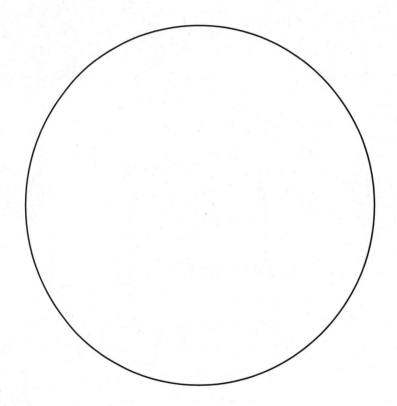

Story: _____

I learned to read a new word.

Here it is _____

Name: _____

Date: _____

Newsletter

A World of Animals

Dear Family,

Our last reading theme for the year will be *A World of Animals*. All of the Read Aloud and Big Book stories children will listen to are about animals. Children will focus on recognizing and writing the letter *j* and also identify the sound it represents.

Theme-Related Activities to Do Together

The Letters *Jj*

With pieces of string and a dime, form both a capital and a lower case letter *j*, and have your child identify the letters. Together think of words that start like the word *jog*.

Guess That Number

Page through animal picture books when you play Guess That Number. First guess how many animals are on a page. Then check each guess by counting the number of animals.

Animal Collages

Together cut out newspaper pictures of different animals and paste them onto a sheet of paper. Help your child label the picture with the correct animal names.

Theme-Related Books to Enjoy Together!

I Had a Hippopotamus *by Hector Viveros Lee. Lee & Low 1998 (32p) also paper* A boy imagines what he would do with the creatures in his box of animal crackers. Available in Spanish as *Yo tenía un hipopótamo.*

Harry the Dirty Dog *by Gene Zion. Harper 1956 (32p) also paper* This is a classic story about a dog, some dirt, and a bath. Available in Spanish as *Harry, el perrito sucio.*

The Bossy Gallito *by Lucia M. Gonzalez. Scholastic 1999 (32p) also paper* A bossy rooster learns a lesson about politeness in this cumulative Cuban folktale. *Text in English and Spanish.*

Nuts to You! *by Lois Ehlert. Harcourt 1993 (32p)* A frisky squirrel digs up bulbs, steals birdseed, and enters a house through a tear in a screen.

Coyote *by Gerald McDermott. Harcourt (32p) also paper* Coyote persuades some crows to help him fly in this Native American trickster tale. Available in Spanish as *Coyote.*

Sweet Dreams *by Kimiko Kajikawa. Holt 1999 (32p)* Simple rhyming verse paired with photographs describes the many different ways animals sleep.

Boletín

Animales del mundo

Estimada familia:

El último tema de lectura de este año es *Animales del mundo*. Todos los cuentos en los libros de lectura en voz alta (Read Aloud stories) y en los libros grandes (Big Books) son acerca de animales. Los niños aprenderán a reconocer y a escribir la letra *j* y a identificar el sonido que representa esa letra.

Actividades para hacer juntos

La letra *Jj*

Forme una *j* mayúscula y una minúscula con pedazos de cordel y una moneda, y pida a su niño que identifique las letras. Juntos piensen en palabras que comiencen con el sonido de la letra *j*, como la palabra *jugo*.

A adivinar el número

Hojéen un libro de dibujos o fotos de animales mientras juegan "Adivina cuántos hay". Primero traten de adivinar cuántos animales hay en una página. Luego cuenten los animales en cada página para verificar.

Montajes de colores

Recorten dibujos o fotos del periódico que sean de un mismo color y péguenlos en una hoja de papel. Ayude a su niño o niña a escribir en la hoja de papel el nombre del color que escogieron.

Libros relacionados al tema que pueden leer juntos

I Had a Hippopotamus *por Hector Viveros Lee. Lee & Low 1998 (32p) disponible como libro de bolsillo* Un niño que tiene un caja de galletas en forma de animales se imagina lo que haría con ellos. Disponible en español con el título *Yo tenía un hipopótamo.*

Harry the Dirty Dog *por Gene Zion. Harper 1956 (32p) disponible como libro de bolsillo* Este es un cuento clásico acerca de un perro sucio y del baño que le da un niño. Disponible en español con el título *Harry, el perrito sucio.*

The Bossy Gallito *por Lucia M. Gonzalez. Scholastic 1999 (32p) disponible como libro de bolsillo* Un gallo mandón aprende una lección acerca de los buenos modales en este cuento tradicional cubano. El texto del libro aparece en inglés y en español.

Nuts to You! *por Lois Ehlert. Harcourt 1993 (32p)* Una ardilla inquieta desentierra bulbos, roba y entra en una casa por el agujero de una alambrera.

Coyote *por Gerald McDermott. Harcourt (32p) disponible como libro de bolsillo* En este cuento clásico, Coyote convence a algunos cuervos a que le ayuden a volar. Disponible en español con el título *Coyote.*

Sweet Dreams *por Kimiko Kajikawa. Holt 1999 (32p)* Fotos y versos sencillos en rima, describen las muy distintas maneras en que duermen los animales.

Theme 10

Name _____   Date _____

	Beginning	Developing	Proficient
Listening Comprehension • Participates in shared and choral reading			
• Listens to story attentively			
Phonemic Awareness • Blends, segments phonemes			
• Substitutes phonemes			
• Idenitifies beginning sound			
Phonics • Recognizes sound for *j*			
• Builds words with word families *-ug, -ut*			
Concepts of Print • Uses a capital at the beginning of a sentence			
• Uses end punctuation (period, question mark, exclamation mark)			
Reading • Reads simple texts			
• Reads the high-frequency words *are, he*			
Comprehension • Identifies story beginning, middle, and end			
• Can compare and contrast story elements			
• Recognizes plot (problem, solution)			
Writing and Language • Writes simple phrases or sentences			
• Participates in shared and interactive writing			

For each child, write check marks or notes in the appropriate columns.

Rebus pictures for sentence building

My Journal

Name

hot

cold

Science Center Activity

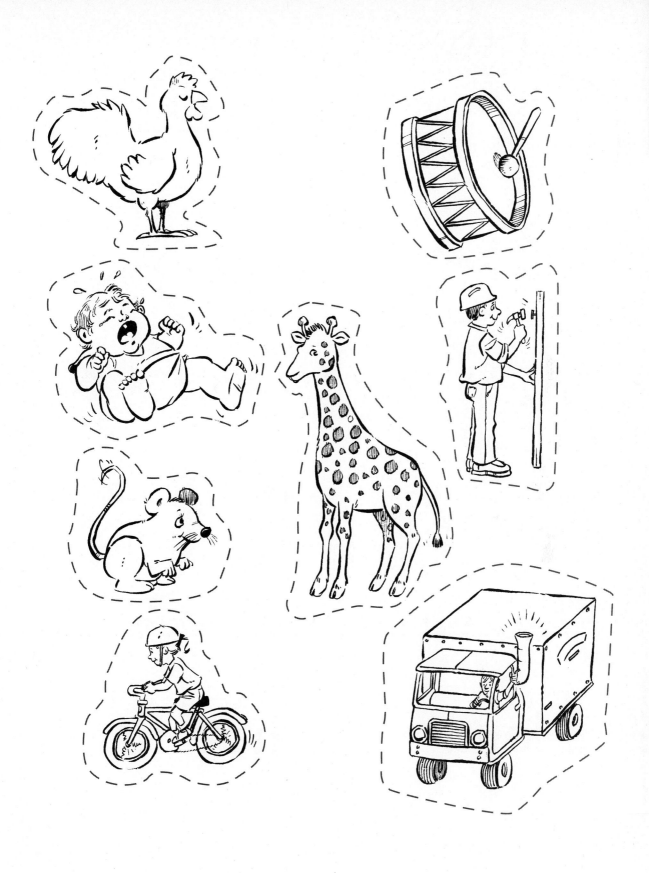

loud | not loud

Story retelling props for *The Tale of the Three Little Pigs*

Story retelling props for *The Tale of the Three Little Pigs*

Story retelling props for *Henny Penny*

I read a new book today!

Name: _____

Date: _____

HANDWRITING

Ball and Stick Alphabet		Continuous Stroke Alphabet	
Aa		Aa	
Letter	Page	Letter	Page
Aa	157	Aa	183
Bb	158	Bb	184
Cc	159	Cc	185
Dd	160	Dd	186
Ee	161	Ee	187
Ff	162	Ff	188
Gg	163	Gg	189
Hh	164	Hh	190
Ii	165	Ii	191
Jj	166	Jj	192
Kk	167	Kk	193
Ll	168	Ll	194
Mm	169	Mm	195
Nn	170	Nn	196
Oo	171	Oo	197
Pp	172	Pp	198
Qq	173	Qq	199
Rr	174	Rr	200
Ss	175	Ss	201
Tt	176	Tt	202
Uu	177	Uu	203
Vv	178	Vv	204
Ww	179	Ww	205
Xx	180	Xx	206
Yy	181	Yy	207
Zz	182	Zz	208

Name: _____

Writing the Alphabet

Aa

A A A

a a a

Writing the Alphabet

Name: _____

B B B

b b b

Name: _____

Writing the Alphabet

Cc

C C C

c c c

Dd

Writing the Alphabet

Name: _____

D D D

d d d

Ee

Name: _____

E E E

e e e

Ff

Name: _____

F F F

f f f

Gg

Name: _____

G G G

g g g

Hh

Writing the Alphabet

Name: _____

H H H

h h h

I i

Writing the Alphabet

Name: _____

I I I

I I I

i i i

Name: _____

J j

J J J J J

j j j j j

Kk

Writing the Alphabet

Name: _____

K K K

k k k

Ll

Writing the Alphabet

Name: _____

Name: _____

Mm

MMM

mmm

Nn

Writing the Alphabet

N N N

n n n

Writing the Alphabet

Oo

Pp

Writing the Alphabet

P P P

p p p

Name: _____

Qq

Q Q Q

q q q

Name: _____

Rr

R R R

r r r

Ss

Name: _____

S S S

s s s

Name: _____

Writing the Alphabet

T T T

t t t

Uu

Writing the Alphabet

Name: _____

U U U

u u u

Name: _____

Writing the Alphabet

Vv

V V V

V V V

Name: _____

Writing the Alphabet

Ww

W W W

w w w

Writing the Alphabet

Xx

Name: _____

Yy

Y Y Y

Y Y Y

Zz

Writing the Alphabet

Z Z Z

Z z z

Name: _____

Aa

A A A

a a a

Writing the Alphabet

Name: _____

B B B

b b b

Name: _____

Cc

C C C

c c c

Writing the Alphabet

Name: _____

D D D

d d d

E E E

e e e

Ff

Name: _____

F F F

f f f

Gg

Name: _____

G G G

g g g

Hh

Writing the Alphabet

Name: _____

H H H

h h h

Name: _____

Writing the Alphabet

I I I

i i i

Writing the Alphabet

Name: _____

Kk

Name: _____

K K K

k k k

Name: _____

L l

L L L

l l l

Name: _____

M m

M M M

m m m

Name: _____

Writing the Alphabet

Nn

$N N N$

$n\, n\, n$

Name: _____

Writing the Alphabet

Oo

O O O

o o o

Name: _____

Pp

p p p

p p p

Name: _____

Qq

Q Q Q

q q q

Writing the Alphabet

Name: _____

R R R

r r r

Name: _____

Ss

S   S   S

s   s   s

Tt

Writing the Alphabet

Name: _____

T T

t t t

Uu

Name: _____

U U U

u u u

Writing the Alphabet

Vv

V V V

V V V

Name: _____

Ww

WWW

uuu

Name: _____

Writing the Alphabet

Xx

X X X

x x x

Name: _____

Yy

Xx

yyy

Zz

Name: _____

Z z

Z Z Z

z z z